SWIMMING IN THE FLOOD

Later, he would see her on the screen,
trying to smile, as they lifted her on to the dock,

and he'd notice the frame again, baroque and absurd,
and empty, like the faces of the drowned.

SCIENCE

Sound waves were never explained
to my satisfaction,

how they could travel through water, lacing the pool
with muffled voices,

or streaming away from the deep end, to fledge the
     walls
with faint harmonics, lapping semitones.

On Thursdays I went from school
to the public baths

and waited for the body I desired:
the swallow dive, the underwater glide,

the surface tension
of a second skin.

In physics I watched a light beam shatter and heal,
bleeding to crimson and blue in a prism of glass,

and wondered if a soul could change like that,
my father's shadow filtered through the lens

and disappearing, leaving something clean
and weighted, like the swimmer's earned fatigue,

rhythmic and steady,
a sine wave of grace and attunement.

A DISTANT COUSIN

I thought I could track you down
to one of those straw-covered huts
in Pittencrieff Park:
hairless and cicatriced, you would crouch in the rain,
gone native in the drip of rhododendrons.

Or, naked as bats in flight, we would meet in the ferns,
merging, then wheeling away
to the family outing:
my mother under her headscarf, smudged with mascara,
lining the others in rows for the Instamatic.

I thought I would find you submerged
in a hidden pool,
breathing through water, waiting to capture my soul,
the way our pictures only caught the forced
rehearsal of a smile, a milk-toothed grin,
the hint of a suspicion in our eyes
that someone was at home, while we were gone,
misting the windows, veiling the mirrors with stour.

WRONG

I

A swallowed nail. A trick with razor blades.

Round the allotments, four in the afternoon,
October: I was gouging out a face,
a jack-a-lantern's grin of candlelight,
the jagged mouth, the nose, the death's-head eyes,
my knife too sharp, too reverently held

– that was my shed, my bunker, that smell of grease
and sacking, shrivelled tubers, rows of shrouded jars,
permethrin and flowers of sulphur,
phoxim and derris, rat poison's prussic blues,

a six by eight descent into the dark
where all I wanted was a raptor's grace,
an undertaker's skill with flesh and bone,
a single-mindedness, a sense of being.

II

Leaving the tattered parade
of bandsmen and footballers' wives,

and the clowns with their greasepaint smiles
and their buckets of silver,

I crossed the park
and found a borderline:

a wet sun, a muddy horizon,
cows standing out in a pasture

of thistles and dung.
For years I've wondered how it all went wrong,

how I went down,
how gulped air thickened to milk,

and how I was drained by that other
who found me there,

fluttering over my face
like a giant bat,

holding the knife that would cut through my flesh
like butter, then letting me fall

and turning away to the crowd
where he disappeared.

The rest like the far side of gas, that improbable
blue that dissolved, when I woke in the dentist's chair,

and a scatter of coins on the grass
in a cobweb of blood

red as the carnival mouths
of the drum majorettes

moving away
to the quiet erasure of distance.

III

I prayed for my father's death
on Sundays, when he mowed his patch of lawn,
his half-mad collie yapping at his heels,
his wife in the kitchen, snivelling over the onions.
I sat in our apple tree, hidden among the leaves,
my kneecaps and thumb-knuckles
crocheted with moss and bark
and willed him dead – the wish not mine alone,
but something of the house that drew me in:
that substance they found one winter, tucked in the flue,
all shinbone and whiskers, and nothing they could have
    named
with its winglike arms and a blue, almost questioning face,
a stitchwork of horsehair and mortar to hold it together,
mislaid all its life in a gap between snowfalls and cinders.

IV

There were small things I killed for pleasure:
ladybirds, craneflies, spiders and night-flying moths,
stubbing them out with my fingers
on icy glass,
or filling a jar with bees, to watch them
flicker and die.
I sprinkled lines of salt
on worms and slugs
and waited for the larger, sweeter kills:
the neighbour's Siamese, tied in a sack
and bubbling under the stream of Cotter's brook,
the poisoned owls, the dog lying dead in the road
– a logic that brings me here, to this neck of the woods
where no one will find him for days: a luckless child,
staring through water and leaves, and a remnant of warmth
bleeding away to the absence of love and mother.

V

I know this scene by heart:
the card from the victim arrives
from Margate or Clacton,
the voice-over comes through a blur
of milk-floats and Radio 1,
but the child is already dead
in a shallow grave,
a wet face covered with leaves,
the blue of his eyes
a promise for rats and magpies.
Then cut to an empty field
in a misty dawn,
the splash in the ditch, the headlamps,
the passing car –
I know he is only a prop
but I watch for a likeness,
that boy-child who's haunted the film
from the first bleak shot,
the photograph, the carnival parade
– and I think of his family
leaning to touch the screen
and find him again
or taste what they knew all along
was waiting to happen:
that sweetness that feathers the tongue;
that sense of themselves
as seen, like the people in movies.

A FOLK STORY

Sometimes I wake in the night
and see her by the light my window casts,
a thin white girl with blisters on her skin,
eternally punished, gathering fistfuls of pain
beyond the canal,

or when the meadow creeps in through my fence,
I find her, on some weekday afternoon,
standing alone, bare-legged, in a pool
of venom.   She is the one
condemned to gather nettles,
wading the banks and ditches, brushing the leaves
with hesitant fingers, unable to grasp the stems
or reach down through the dark, to pull the roots
and step out from the circle of her hurt
into the cool of the day and the green smell of docken.

This could become a pleasure:
plucking the nettles and letting the poison creep
through her fingers and wrists,
bracelets of heat and numbness
binding her skin to the earth,
the finest hair continued through the roots
to gravity.

       Her sin is nothing more
than lightness, like a child's attempt to fly,
a glimpse of swallows feeding on the wing,
a tendency to follow thistledown,

and later she will miss the undergrowth,
this swim in pain and darkness for the taste
of something in the distance, black as loam,
or dock leaves, an arm's-length away, in the cool of the
    hedgerow,
soothing as milk, or a borehole of thawglass and water.

THE LIGHT INSTITUTE

I was an extra, walking home alone
in a matinée rain,

vaguely aware of the church, and the hunting owls
on Stenhouse Street, the house-of-horror bats

circling the lamps, a sub-fluorescent dust
of popcorn and velour, sprinkled on my clothes

like spots of light.
                          Mother was Myrna Loy
in the empty kitchen,

standing at the centre of the world
with flour on her hands, in a halo of musk and steam,

and someone else was coming from the gold
of infinite distance, someone I would know

from memory: the master of the house,
plugged into the undertow of scripts

where I could happen, suddenly alive,
chosen for something, leaving my bed in the dark

and crossing the yard to meet him on the far
border of knowledge and skill,

the hero now, the one I should have been:
Walter Pidgeon. Gable. Franchot Tone.

HOME MOVIE

They are one generation away
from Gaelic, or Latin,
walking the orchards in spray suits and surgical masks,
their science-fiction bodies catch the light
or thicken and set in the shadows, like evening dew,

and I am the one who has come
from the distant city,
stumbling upon their magic, their ram's heads and candles,
the singing at midnight, the dance on the moonlit green,
their stubborn games
of death and resurrection.

I should have left the village reels ago:
as soon as I met the children on the cliffs
I should have guessed – that laughter in the grass,
their knowing looks, the whispers in their sleeves.
I should have listened when the doctor spoke,
clumsy and fearful, barring the surgery door,
and when his body washed up on the rocks
covered with stings and bruises, I should have known.

Now I am packing my bags in an upstairs room
while, somewhere below, the solstice is set to begin.
I still intend to take the next train out
– as soon as the midwife comes, in her starched white dress
to give me her blessing: an apple; a copper nail;
a name from the churchyard;
the dead in their cradles of drowning.

HYPOTHESIS

Let this be home: the house we never had,
a box of lights, a jar of copper nails,
cats' bones and feathers
an arm's length into the chimney.

Deep in the garden
the edges wander and blur,
convolvulus winds through the roses, the violets drift,
spotting the ditches with colour beyond the canal.

Some nights, the fox slips by
in the blood-orange light,
leaving his kill: the wet pelt, the rot-threaded eyes,
the bones in the ceanothus, becoming dust,

and waking will sometimes resemble
the sudden precision of gunshots out in the field,
when the woods are immersed
in a clear and improbable dawn,

and traces everywhere of what is risen:
bonemeal and horsehair, a fingerprint etched in the dust,
whatever it is that fades when we enter a room,
leaves only the glitter of brass, and the gloved noise of
    water.

ASCENSION DAY

Your neighbours on Borrowdale Road
are listening in,

as if they have found the gap
between Light and Third

where summer begins
in a shortfall of dust and feathers.

I'm standing in your kitchen,
late for school,

loaded with books in French and the unexpected
gravity of apple cores and ink

and the hush of your mother's voice
that keeps starting again

as she travels from room to room
in the wide upstairs

– something about the summer
and being friends –

emerging through birdsong and traffic
like Patsy Cline.

A MIRACLE ON MARKET DAY

In the graveyard it's evening already,
four in the afternoon, the lamps lit too early,
yellow and soft as gas
in the summer air.
The trees are still. A girl in a cotton dress
is raising the dead,
peeling the turf back, lifting them out of their graves
and setting them on their feet with a gentle shove
to start them in motion.
                        Some have already
wandered as far as the gate,
weak as kittens, blind in the common light,
they stand on the pavement, blinking; unsure of themselves
they stare at the palms of their hands, find smudges of loam,
the smell of old water, the sweetness of wasp-pitted apples.
Back in the churchyard, the twilight thickens and spreads,
the girl moves on, so innocent of will
she might be an angel.
The market is one bright flag
of headscarfs and shrouds.
Out here it is daylight. We cannot believe what we see.

THE SEXTON'S DAUGHTER

I slept in my father's blood
till the day I was born:
poker-faced, eyeless, he buried my voice in the pond,
and set me amongst the kingcups
to watch for a sign.

When nothing appeared, I learned how to breathe
    underwater,
how bodies are resurrected
through fish-skin and mud
and how the wings are hidden in the flesh
when the angel descends to Mary – a common man
demanding the usual agreement, expecting no answer.

At twelve I returned. I could still feel his hands in my dress
in the cool of the day,
and Mother was a song I never learned,
eternally virgin, lost in the bandwidths of summer,
moving from child to child in the church marquee,
dispensing a vague and unexpected love.

At night I would climb to the attic
to see him nude:
bear-shaped and senseless, he harrowed me under the sheets,
while I moved on, through reeds and irises,
to where my voice was floating on the lake,
brighter than silver, threaded with water and venom,
drawn to his whimpers and cries, like a Halloween moon.

CATCH-KISS

A scrap of memory: I'm six years old,
it's dark, it's hot, there's someone in my room.
I'm rubbing out the man I used to draw,
the clubfoot at the corner of the page
with scary eyes.
I'm rubbing out the interrupted park,
that no-man's-land beyond the public baths,
its cinemas and minor industries,
buttonmakers, chapels of repose.
His hands are cold. He makes me close my eyes
then lift my skirt and promise not to tell.
I'm eight years old. It's warm. The sun's too bright.
I'm rubbing out the girl I used to draw,
her awkward love, her feigned incompetence.
I've found a better colour for her dress,
a blue in the middle-distance that might be fog,
an endless four o'clock of light and snow.
I fill the house with robins' eggs and stars,
yellow ochre, jars of sticklebacks.
You'll find them in the picture: faded stains,
traces, relics, shreds of understanding.
Sometimes he held my face and made me drink.
His friend was there. He said I'd been asleep.
I've found a place for mother in the yard:
you'll see her later, standing by the tree.
I'll draw this girl again: her yellow dress,
her way of staying hidden till the last.
I'll draw the room, an attic in the roof
where someone else – a girl I ought to know –
is calling softly, crying in the dark,
waiting to be released
from her buckled sleeves.

LACK OF EVIDENCE

I

The woods in the slow fade of evening.
In the four hundred yards
from the bus to her own front gate,
she disappeared,

gone into snowberries, frostfall,
the song of thrushes;
gone into a stranger's
measured voice.

They found a cardigan, a pair of shoes;
a felt-tip pen; a box of paper clips.
Did no one see her vanish in the grass,
leaving behind this stain, like a chanterelle?

The body they pulled from the brook
matched no description:
Katrina: twelve years old; brown hair; blue eyes.
Quiet spoken. Pretty. Always smiling.

II

We are pure souls, buried in flesh,
traces of ether, hanging in a web
of blood and hair,
immersed in muscle, pinned to gravity.
Our life is penance. Death is our release:
ascending through a mist of atmospherics,
faint as the dwindling echo of Creation.

I saw her walking home, that autumn day,
still innocent, still lit with God's intent.
She looked so beautiful, I set her free:
a moment's work, to peel away the skin
and let the spirit flutter through my hands.

I said a prayer and laid her in the stream.
She touched my face. Our hearts were joined in silence.

III

Her room is as it was
the day she left:
I change the linen, draw the blinds at night,
hoover and dust
the way I always did.
Nothing has changed. It's all immaculate.

Sometimes I meet the bus
she would be on,
then walk home through the woods, taking the path
she would have taken, looking for the clues
the policemen missed.
I found a bracelet once. It wasn't hers.

Her father broods. Her sister cries at night.
There's something in our lives
will not be eased:
a flaw in time, a blemish on the air.
This pain is like a cage we cannot leave.
We bear it well and will not let it be.

SCHADENFREUDE

How I suspected myself
of someone else,
when they caught me out by the kilns
with Sandra Gillespie,
reaching through zips and buttons for the damp
plumage of her undecided flesh,

and when I was far in the heat
of a May afternoon,
wading through duckweed and balsam to raid the nests
of moorhens and coots,
I knew in my secret heart
I was up to no good

and relished the inexplicable
malice of being,
holding the eggs in my mouth while I climbed the fence,
or crouched to our delicate barter, finding her out
through a vapour of perfume and salt
and the smoothing of cotton.

AN ORDERED WORLD

For a long time they still believed
in the presence of ether

and relics of angels,
floating in infinite space:

traces of radium,
knuckles and slivers of light,

a milky drift
of hydrogen and stars.

They listened for the hiss of radio
and animals that lingered in the flesh,

the origin of things, the coming end,
a god's withdrawal, fading in the mind.

They worked for years in cool herbaria
unravelling the filmy ferns and palms;

in dark menageries, they measured
wingspan, proboscis, angle of tooth and claw,

returning at night to assemblies
of bright apparatus

to find the algebraic fingerprint
that must be there, the way the soul exists

though nothing ever draws it from the web
of meat and fat: a voiced uncertainty,

a shadow on the finest instruments,
vestigial, demonic, inexact.

A SWIMMING LESSON

Maybe it's luck, or a talent for going naked
that lets one body mingle with the stream
till fingers and eyes and even the lungs
are water. Maybe it's a gift
for transformation,
changing from child to swan at the river's edge,
from swan to fish, from fish to waterweed.
And maybe it's a pledge to gravity
that keeps another wedded to the earth,
the way I would dive to prove the riverbed
before I could swim midstream,
probing the mud with my fingers, clawing up handfuls
of pebbles and silt, and drowned bodies
eased from their bones
– I had to know that solid ground was there,
while she was drifting, merging with the tide,
taking a form from the water and making it hers,
accepting its favours, repaying the debt in kind.

In my dream you are sitting out
at the edge of the water,
watching me wade towards you in the dark:
time has stood still since the river
leached out the last thread of warmth and left you to dry,
the blue of your lips, the strawberry-red of your mouth,
a lure for the boys who found you, a lifetime away.
In my dream I am lifting the eyes from your milky skull
and I'm placing these pebbles of glass in the empty sockets
to see if they'll quicken and heal in your salvaged flesh.

She lived at the far end of town.
After the lesson, she'd leave me and wander away
through coal-black woods beyond the railway yards

where men and dogs were hunting in the grass,
drawing their secret kills from a web of static.
I never went that far, I always stopped,
though sometimes I thought I was there, in my scarf and
    gloves,
standing out under an elm tree, watching the shadows
flare from my torch beam, up in the higher boughs.
There were houses out there, there were rooms filled with
    spiders and damp
where children could go for a dare and be unreturned,
– empty blouses, sandals, cotton socks –
and ten yards into the bushes, a holy well
that was only a puddle of mud and clouded rain,
where Ellen MacInnes was brushed by a sand-coloured
    wing
and wandered home pregnant.

Waiting for you to step
like a heron out of the slow
green river,
I watched the reed beds
darken with a long caressing wind,
and wondered what we leave
beneath the silt,
footprints and tangles of hair
that will sink forever,
that bracelet you once let fall
through the streaming weeds
– diving for almost an hour, we came up
empty-handed, feeling it settle and drift,
like the bodies we shed
when we hoist ourselves on to the bank,
moving away for good
in a skin's depth of water.

She swam in the dark and the light,
but midnight was what she knew
like the warp of her mind,
the cattle gathered round to watch her rise,
the smell of the trees, the leaf-melt that clung to her fingers
– so it was dawn when they found her
somewhere downriver,
a nakedness for everyone to share,
boys on the footpath,
policemen with hooks and lines
– and I'd choose to remember
a country of mile-deep woods,
shoals of fishes hanging in the streams
like coloured flags, and my shadow swimming away
on a field of barley,
but all I can see is the mud in the lines of her face,
and the scatter of leaves
that someone has brushed aside,
revealing the clouded skin, and the gas–blue eyes
where thinking has stopped,
like the calm at the edge of a snowfall.

IN THE PSYCHIATRIC HOSPITAL

This was a private house
in other times:
thumbprints smudging the walls
in the day room;
cat-hairs and traces of perfume
sealed in the paintwork like pledges:
a ghost forensic.
Now there are stockyards and marshes
in every bed,
women laid out in flannel and medication,
meeting their fathers again, after thirty years,
fumbling with buttons, bleeding away through their dreams,
and men who have drowned on land
a thousand times,
drowning again, in a vapour of chalk and water,
a little in love with the pain
they have come here to mend.
At night I can hear the owls
in the neighbouring fields,
feel them glide and circle in the dark,
a slow waltz
of grace and correction.
At night there is something
scratches in the wall,
a damp-haired panic,
swaddled in copper and gypsum.
Sometimes it cries and I rise in the blue of the ward,
crossing the moon-squared chessboard of the floor
to press my hands to where I heard it last,
finding the hollow, finding the gap in my thoughts,
feeling the pulse rise, quick,
through the blood in my fingers.

CATHY

I

She said she had buried the doll
where no one would find it,
then dreamed of its hidden face: the cherry mouth,
the baby-blue eyes, the thumbnails, the crinkled hair;
those words she had written in ink
on its chest and thighs.
It had a voice, she said: a length of string,
a root she could feel tearing loose, when she made it talk,
and there was something birdlike in the way
it lay unmoving when she closed the box,
the way it had folded wings beneath the dress,
and how it would feel the cold, in the frozen earth,
or moulder slowly, drenched in years of rain,
keeping its secret intact, in a voicebox of iron.

II

She listens to space: the motion of the stars,
the various forms of carbon, sputniks and dust,
gas-clouds and signals, scorched in the heat of the sun;
and someone is there — a version of herself,
nostalgic for the earth, the formal lawns,
the buddleia, the pull of gravity.
She has to keep this conversation
running: when the mist is in the woods,
whenever the pond in the rose garden
freezes, she must whisper through a fog
of radio, to one who sometimes shifts,
is somewhere else in that infinity,
tuned to another soul, as yet unborn,
a purer mind, a cleaner way of seeing.

She walks up the sunlit hill
past ECT
to where the workshop stands
in a tangle of briars.
The smell of paint in cakes and dried-up jars
reminds her of school: those whispers of sex and romance
that made the world a promise and a danger.
Her artwork pools and seeps into the desk;
she lets it bleed, watching the colours run,
then walks to the open door to taste the air,
her memory a shroud of names and fears
that someone unravels and gives her, from time to time,
bewildering, but still a perfect fit,
a garment of presence whose purpose she cannot fathom.

A PRIVATE LIFE

I want to drive home in the dusk
of some late afternoon,

the journey slow, the tractors spilling hay,
the land immense and bright, like memory,

the pit towns smudges of graphite,
their names scratched out for good: Lumphinnans;

Kelty. I want to see
the darkened rooms, the cups and wireless sets,

the crimson lamps across the playing fields,
the soft men walking home through streets and parks

and quiet women, coming to their doors,
then turning away, their struck lives gathered around them.

SUMMER

When the heat fades
the dog-fox returns,
tracing an earlier path along the lane,
a glimmer of self
in the mazework of blood and urine.
The pine trees are still.
From village to village you hear
the same dull murmur of bees
and the shiver that quickens the hedge
is only the wind,

but tonight we could almost believe
in fairies: how they surface through the grass
or drift through the kitchen,
stitching our milk with venom,
tonight they are almost here, though nothing is here
but the day's warmth, fading away
through brickwork and skin
and the rice-paper ghost of the moon on an open field
where the barn owl descends
to a parish of barley and nettles.

A STOLEN CHILD

My father would say
I belonged to someone else:
the fairies had come in the night, invading his house
with spells, and the mouse-smell of hemlock.

And I would go out at dusk
to the edge of the world,
finding the snow-flavoured gaps
in the swimming barley
and searching for the palace of the king

who might be disguised as a tramp, in an old black coat,
bobbing for mice and hedgehogs in the weeds
and changing them into the semblance
of children, to fill his house
with pockets of warmth, like games for the cold to enjoy.

BURNING A WOMAN

I   WITCH WIFE

Sooner or later, you know she will make a spell
to feel the devil simmer in her flesh,

the moment of her pleasure incandescent:
foreign spirits burning in the dark

while others sleep. A woman in the house
is partly a hostage to fortune

and partly your mirror
shaken and brought to life

and no matter how often you try
to draw the thread of brightness from a son's

water and buttermilk skin,
his mother's language trickles off his tongue

and he stands in the yard like a girl
while you bring in the cattle,

snuffling and giggling,
calling each heifer by name.

II CARDIAC

My father is standing tall
in our narrow kitchen:

blood on the table,
a litter of eggs and glass

on the clouded floor.
He's clutching a fistful of coins

like a drowning swimmer,
drunk again, and dead these seven years,

but still, in my frightened dreams,
immersed in anger;

looking for someone to blame
that he might be pardoned

and go down under the flood
with his heart intact.

I liked how he said it, as if it were
honey, or dew,
or something you drank with the ladies:
a secret pleasure.
It made me believe he had come
from another language,
with names for the colour of pines
in the morning sun
or how a woman smells when giving birth,
and no historic past
or future tense,
only a present of streetlamps and empty roads,
and men spilling out of the light, in the evening air,
or wandering into the blue
of a different story.

Let me imagine you capable of love
and transformation,

the dream of a man made subtle, or straight as a die,
a judge of character, a connoisseur,

whatever you thought you had lost, when you made me
listen for years to stories I couldn't believe.

I know how you shift and start when I'm passing the time,
walking from church to church in a foreign city,

making coffee, talking on the phone,
clumsy, helpless, sorry for myself,

and just the man you wanted me to be,
good for nothing, skilled in self-deceit,

punished so often for errors I never made
I'm blind to my worst mistakes, and beyond redemption.

V BURNING A WOMAN

A dark afternoon. The houses on Eastwood Road
are Belgian, all of a sudden,
where someone has lit a fire in a corner of privet;

damp and slow, a fleece of yellow smoke
clings to the leaves like mildew; I think of the time
my father stood in the yard at Handcross Court

burning my mother, a fortnight after she died:
her only coat, her witch's broom of scarves,
bonnets and nylons, ribbons of freshwater pearls.

I've worked from this faded blueprint and got it wrong
time after time,
thinking I see him wandering back and forth,

trailing dresses, stoking the fire with shoes
to watch them burn,
then seeing myself, next morning in the rain,

probing the ashes for salvage, for hairpins and beads,
a litter of buttons, like eggs going cold in the nest,
or the précis of stitchwork and feathers she once made
    good.

SEARCHING FOR LAMBS

As I walked out one May morning,
One May morning betime,
I met a maid, from home had strayed,
Just as the sun did shine.

I sometimes wonder if the girl was real,
or was she just an echo from the walls,
my own invention, hatched from bricks and dust?
We might have passed each other on the stairs,
or breathed the same damp air
beneath the roof,
where startled thrushes fluttered through the beams
and vanished
in the smoky undergrowth.

She might have been a ghost when she appeared,
coming from nowhere, fledged with the falling light,
and something about the place
had made me wild,
the smell of the cisterns,
the traces of ash and carbon.

Later she lay beneath me, vaguely unreal,
like those root crops you sometimes find
on a greengrocer's stall
– carrots and parsnips, with stubbed legs and private parts,
and whiskers around the cracks
like pubic hair.
I pulled down her crumpled dress
to cover the whiteness.

That was a lifetime ago, but I see her now,
fluttering under my hands, like a wounded bird,

and I know, if I could,
I would step back and let her pass,
walking away through the trees, with the sun on her hair,
holding intact
the beauty I wanted to fathom.

NATALIE

I

She wanted a house in the country
near Stonham Parva:
a pink house, with birds in the garden,
junipers, beehives, a horseshoe to hang on the door.
She would marry in haste.
She wanted a car she could drive
to Ipswich, or Yarmouth,
glimpses of alien lives
through a living-room window
and, later, the absolute cold
of the possible ghost,
where attic lights were golden in the dark,
and distant, like beauty, or love, or a sense of herself,
almost impossible, always about to begin.

She bled through the noise of the sea.
A last hour of pain and dismay
on a public beach.
The endless stars, the wonder of it all,
the taste of salt, the pebbles in her coat
dwindling away, as a stranger took what he wanted,
then more, and left her
boneless in the sand.
At dawn she was found near the pier
by a man and his dog,
blue as a jellyfish, maculate, stripped to the waist,
looking as if there was something she wanted to say,
her mouth struck open, choking on the gag,
smudged with detergent, blood-bruises, blisters of laver.

THE OLD GODS

Now they are condemned
to live in cracks,
in bubbles of plaster and rust,
and spiders' webs
behind the furniture:

speaking a derelict language
to empty space,
sealed with the vapour
in bottles, closed in the blown
robins' eggs
in some abandoned loft.

Each has its given power.
Each has its hearth, its secret,
its local name,
and each has its way of learning
the skill of return,
the science of bleeding through, when anger or fear
is fuzzing the surface,
making us dizzy and whole.

BARREN

This is where babies are found:
on riverbanks, amongst the mud and rushes,
eggy and silent, gazing through empty water.
Her body is cold and free: she remembers the spells,
the singsong she used to hear in her mother's kitchen.
She walks three times around a moonlit lake,
gathers a man root, wears it against her throat,
fashions a doll from wax and the pollen of lilies.
When nothing works, she turns to something else:
a silver coin, a lucky rabbit's foot.
At night she wanders, crossing icy fields,
a starlit body, splashing through the grass
to touch the cattle, blood-warm in their pastures,
laying her face to their sides, to feel the movement,
the purr of the darkness within, and the rich wombs,
    breeding.

SEPTEMBER

The first owls are working the dusk
on the upper field,
flitting back and forth along the hedge,
desultory and conversational
their low-pitched calls,
their sudden dips and turns.
This is a moment's grace, a stepping out
to gloaming, and the first breeze off the hills,
as I stand with my back to the wall
to feel the heat,
and listen, through the river of the trees,
for something of myself that waits to come,
as lyrical and poignant as the sound
of little owls and foxes on the hill
hunting for blood and warmth, in the yellow bracken.

THE RAINBOW

It's only a trick of the light
and nobody's promise

and six months after the flood, he knows how a people
are fooled by their landmarks,

and how they invent them anew, becoming accustomed
to runnels and pools

and the fen smell
of earthworks and ditches.

He'd rather be buried at sea
than drowned on the land,

clutching at rootless trees
and ephemeral houses,

and each time it rains
he remembers his first day home,

wading from stall to stall
in a lather of diesel

and finding the horses
shrouded in duckweed and mud.

His neighbours came
to lay them in the ground

then left him to the locked barometer,
the clock stopped with silt,

the almanac
drowned in the fire.

PAROUSIA

I

I could imagine a biblical presence:
a darkening of matter like this charged
sky, before the coming of the storm,
the lime trees around the station
streaming with rain,
a stiffening, a scab of pus and blood,
a wound on the air, a voice above the rooves,

— but I think, if it came, there would be
something more subtle:
a blur at the corner of vision, a trick of the light,
or the notion that things have shifted

closer: streetlamps and walls,
privet hedges, trees, the neighbour's door,
intimate, all of a sudden, and out in the dark

the animals defined and understood
— vixen and weasel, barn owl and pipistrelle —
granted their privileged moments to sleep and kill.

II

Companion self: not me, but echoes
breeding on the skin;
a half-life of touches and blows, the sub-microscopic
pattern of resurrection.
                              I knew I could squat
in the fen-smell under the hedge
or walk away through fields and timber yards
to moorhens' nests and oildrums full of rain,

but somewhere along the way
I would meet the Christ:
a tripwire; a mat of hair; an open wound;
the silver of fish blood and bone
in the whites of his eyes.

III

There were borders I never crossed:
pools of goldenrod behind the barn,
harrows and tangles of wire
immersed in weed,

the meadow beyond our road, the purple woods,
the watergall, the sub-infinity
of oatfields at dawn

– but I knew he was always present, walking away
in the warmth of the ripening grain,
dangerous, graceful, bright as a circus cat,
or the man from the high wire, come down to touch the
    earth,

tasting the air, how it sweetens and turns to blood
in the throat, in the new-won flesh, in the sudden body.

IV

It was less of a stream than a border:
a rill over wheat-coloured stones, then a sudden
dimming.
         And that was the place to cross,
treading the cold, my bare feet snagging a depth
of fish-skin and weed,
that was the kingdom of pike, where the body was laid
a finger's-depth under the sand.

The far side was stranger's country, a half-mile away:
a back road far in the heat, a gust of wind,
cow parsley, mare's tails, a glimmer of slate in the distance,
and out in the open field, a dog-fox
pausing in its stride, to scent the air,
the only spirit I could understand
the black awareness rooted in its eyes.

A heresy, but soul becomes
conceivable, immersed in viscera,
and mind endures, in wisps of meat and bone;
at twilight, crossing the river, I always knew
something was close, but all I ever saw
was blood-warm, vivid, wholly physical:
the sparrow-hawk sweeping the air, the questing owl,
the stoat in the wall, that knows where its hunger is going.

V

All resurrections are local:
footprints bleeding away
through marsh-grass and water,
a sound you can almost hear
of the flesh renewed
in the plashing of rain
or a quick trout
breaking the stream.

For the sign I have waited to see
is happening now
and always, in this white continuum
of frost and spawn:
the blood in a tangle of thorns
where it stiffens and pales,
the hard bud splitting through ice
and the nailed palm healing.